WE HAVE DONE LIFE TOGETHER

PHILLIP L. MITCHELL

Edited by
NICOLE QUEEN WEBSTER

VPH
VISION PUBLISHING
HOUSE

ISBN: 979-8-9952534-1-9

Vision Publishing House
support@vision-publishinghouse.com
www.vision-publishinghouse.com

This book is established to provide information and inspiration to all readers. It is designed with the understanding that the author is not engaged to render any psychological, legal, or any other kind of professional advice. The content is the sole expression of the author. The author is not liable for any physical, psychological, emotional, financial, or commercial damages, including, but not limited to special, incidental, consequential, or other damages. All readers are responsible for their own choices, actions, and results.

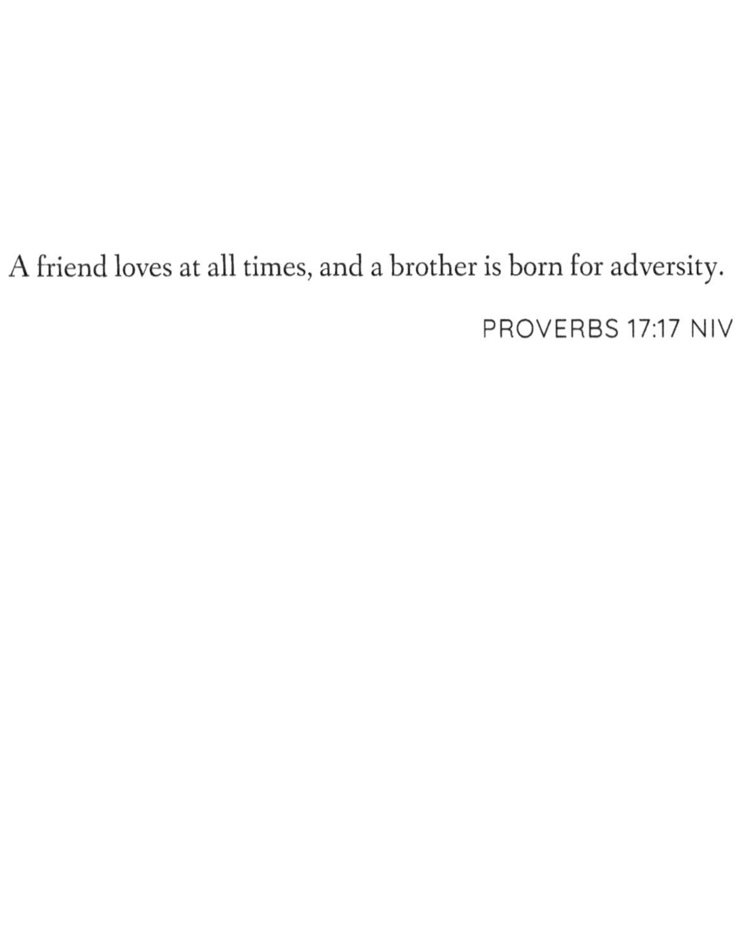

A friend loves at all times, and a brother is born for adversity.

PROVERBS 17:17 NIV

AUTHOR'S NOTE

In 2021, I was sitting in the family room, and I just felt really down. I started thinking about my brother Bill and how he wouldn't be seen the same anymore. At the same time, I was dealing with my own health challenges. Everything hit me all at once, and I just started crying. Right then, I felt the need to think back on all the things we had been through together. Some of it was good. Some of it was hard. That's when the words came to me— *we have done life together*.

I started thinking about the good times we shared and everything we were able to accomplish. People say that writing helps heal the soul, and I believe that's true. At that point in my life, I didn't know how long I had on this earth, and I didn't know how long Bill had either. What I did know was that I wanted other people to know about our journey and the things that brought us to where we are today. I wanted to share the good times, the hard times, and how spirituality can carry you through all of it.

I want this book to be something people can look back on and reflect on—a healing tool. Life has its ups and downs. It has highs, and it definitely has lows. But if you take time to reflect on the good moments, you'll find that there's still joy and laughter in the middle of it all. That's what I hope this book gives you.

This book is for anyone who's ever walked through life with someone by their side. It's for young people from small towns, big cities, the suburbs, and the hood—anyone who can be inspired by two small-town kids trying to make it in life. It's also for people going through health challenges who need a reminder to keep their heads up during hard times. And if you're a caregiver who feels like you don't have an outlet or much support, this book is for you, too.

If you love sports, you'll definitely connect with this story. You'll experience it through the eyes of two young men who had a dream and saw that dream come true. But this book is also for people who reached a dream, lost it all, and realized that starting over is always possible. It's for longtime friends from college, coworkers, and anyone who remembers some of these moments along the way.

And when you really break it down, what I'm really saying is this: this book is for people who have lived some life. If you've shared laughs, tears, setbacks, and victories with people who mattered, and made it through to the other side, this book is for you.

Family is a big part of this story. This book is about having a circle—people who stay when things get rough. People who don't just show up when things are good, but stick around when life gets hard. We're not meant to do life alone. Community matters, and having people around you makes all the difference.

My hope is that you take something real from this book—life lessons, joy, and a sense of togetherness, even when times are tough. No matter what you're facing, we're stronger together. At the end of every chapter, you'll find Coach's Notes. Use them in your everyday life. Share them with your siblings, close friends, church groups, or teams—and talk about them together.

Bill and my relationship started with a love for sports back in high school. But somewhere along the way, we became family. Sports took us places we never thought we'd go and put us in rooms with people we never imagined meeting. You'll read plenty of sports stories in this book, but I want you to look beyond that. Look at the relationship. Look at the family dynamic. Look at the spiritual influence—how God can break you down and still give you life at the same time.

This book talks about life challenges, healing—emotionally and spiritually—mistakes that were made, and the consequences that come with living this thing called life. So yes, this is more than a sports book. It's a life lesson book.

When you finish reading, I hope you realize that life may not be as bad as it sometimes feels. The goal is to reflect, keep a positive outlook for your future, and never give up. So that when you look back just to reflect, you'll see that life still has a lot to offer.

CONTENTS

FOREWORD

Although we were from a large family, Phil and I were both "only" children until one Sunday in 1974. It was on that day that his parents had scheduled a family portrait and needed a girl to complete the family. I was that girl! As we took our "sibling" picture, the photographer said, "Hold your sister's hand!" From that day on, he has been my big brother.

Although he was an only child, he was never alone. There was always someone there, whether it was the Sunday meals his mom provided for college kids from across the state, or the person who just needed a little extra love and support.

In our youth, we were in a play based upon Matthew 25:40: "...Verily I say unto you, Inasmuch as ye have done it unto one of the least of these my brethren, ye have done it unto me."

Phil has lived this verse as his compass throughout his life, and in these pages, it shows.

However, I must admit, when I heard of his 2021 "living arrangement," I was... well, I'm just gonna say it... *pissed!* How was he going to take on this responsibility when he was on dialysis and didn't know what each day would bring for himself?

But later, I realized that to Phil, this was his "assignment." During this time, Phil began to reflect on the milestones that he and Billy experienced together. Although I've heard these stories, reading it and hearing his voice gives their journey new meaning. They truly did life together, and they needed each other, so the title is most fitting!

I invite you to experience their journey as you read these pages. Watch them evolve from high school rivals to fraternity brothers, to coaches, to fathers, and ultimately, to family.

Kim Mitchell Freeman

INTRODUCTION

I invite you to take this journey with Bill and me. It is a journey that began in small towns and eventually led to a big city. It is a story of unfailing love between brothers—a story filled with accomplishments, life challenges, trials, and even failures. The stories shared in this book are lessons we have learned along the way— good, bad, and everything in between. But above all, they are lessons learned.

There were many people who helped us along the way. Many of them will be mentioned in these pages. Several images have been included that capture our memories— moments that may cause some of you to laugh, some to cry, and others simply to reflect and enjoy the journey we have taken.

This book also includes seasons of illness that mirror the deeper challenges of life. It will take you on a sports journey like no other. You may even remember the events we describe. But through my eyes, I want you to see what we saw and experience what we experienced on this journey called life.

As you read, I encourage you to reflect on your own experiences as you learn about ours— our life lessons, the people we loved, and those we lost along the way. It is my hope that by sharing our story, we may help others who are facing their own struggles.

Bill and I were raised in a spiritual home grounded in faith. We want you to view our journey through a biblical lens, while also remembering that we are human—imperfect and capable of mistakes.

So, as you reflect, think of yourself. Embrace each moment. Learn from it. And allow those lessons to help you become a blessing to others, just as Bill and I have been to each other throughout our lives.

1

1966: BORN FOR THE SAME JOURNEY

The year was 1966. The months were August and November. Two boys were born: one in Johnston County and one in Chatham County. They would grow up in neighboring towns. Highway 42 was the road that connected them. Both grew up loving baseball, football, and basketball. One was a die-hard Carolina Tar Heel fan, and the other was a fan of Carolina, State, Duke, and Wake Forest, depending on who was hot in the ACC at the time. We both loved the Georgetown Hoyas and everything John Thompson. One was a Braves fan, and one was a Yankees fan. One was a Raiders fan, and one was a Redskins fan. One was a Lakers fan, and one was a Sixers fan. In other words, we both loved sports.

Growing up was a little different for us. I grew up in a two-parent household with a mother and a father. Billy grew up in a single-parent household with the sweetest mother and the most beautiful sister a guy could ever have. Both of us were well taken care of. We both worked while in high school and had our own cars. We both loved Polo clothes, and one thought that he knew everything about fashion. Life was great for us. Back then we thought we were just two boys on Highway 42. Turns out, God was building a brotherhood that would carry us through championships and challenges.

Coach's Note:

Never underestimate the power of a praying mother and a disciplined father. Foundation is everything.

FALCON PRIDE &
BROTHERHOOD TIES

Billy was born in August of 1966. I was born in November of 1966. That meant that he could start school a year earlier than me. Billy had a year in high school over me. He played basketball at Fuquay-Varina High School. He was a pretty good ballplayer, playing Junior Varsity and Varsity basketball. Coach Larry Senter was his coach. The team he played on was loaded. Some of the guys that I remember from that team were Ron and Don Jones, Thurman Leach, and James Patterson. They were contenders every year.

I played football, basketball, ran track, and played one day of baseball in high school. I failed to mention that Billy and I attended archrival high schools: Clayton High School and Fuquay-Varina High School. I actually started as a freshman for the legendary Coach Glenn Nixon. Billy's football coach at Fuquay was the legendary Coach Graham Myrick. These two coaches were competitors and good friends. Every time they coached against each other, it was an outstanding game.

As a freshman, I started and played in one of the biggest football games between the two schools. It was October 2, 1981. The game was played at Fuquay. It was a night game, and the place was packed.

Once on the field, it did not matter. We were hyped! It came down to a goal line stand and a field goal to win the game. Fuquay had a running back by the name of Daniel Boone. At the goal line, Fuquay gave the ball on 4th down to Daniel Boone. Our defense made a goal line stand. Daniel Boone was not the man that night. (For the younger generation, Google Daniel Boone the TV character.) We marched back down the field for about seventy yards, and David Whitey, our field goal kicker, won the game with a field goal. You would have thought that we had won the Super Bowl. The game was so big that they announced it as the Carolina game the next day. That's how big the rivalry was between the two schools.

This went on for the next three years, with the two teams splitting the games played in almost every sport.

To this day, we always talk about the Fuquay and Clayton rivalry. Even Bill's dad got into the discussion of the rivalry, and he was serious too. Now there are so many high schools between Clayton and Fuquay. Great high school memories.

We met again as freshmen and sophomores in the fall of 1985 at what was then St. Augustine's College, now St. Augustine's University. I was pulling up to the security booth and saw a young man sitting in the booth. If you know anything about St. Augustine's University, you would know that the security booth is a big thing. Most traffic at St. Augustine's University goes through the security checkpoint. As I was driving up to the booth, the young man looked familiar to me. I said, "Hey, I know you!" and he said, "I know you too!" I said, "You from Fuquay Varina?"

This would be the first encounter with this young man from the CAC conference. As a freshman, I really just hung out with freshmen Kevin Cornelius Wright, Kenny Abrom, George McClamb, Jeff Joyner, and Curtis Thornton. We were all one big group like the guys from School Daze.

I would see Billy from time to time on campus as he was majoring in communications. He worked with the famous WAUG radio station, which is one of the first college stations at an HBCU in America.

Billy was always well-dressed and always had a clean haircut. You always knew that he was on campus because he drove a banana-yellow Toyota Celica. Billy was following in the footsteps of my adopted sister and his real sister, Phyllis Lanier. The story has it that Billy's mother, Ms. Joyce, wanted to go to St. Augustine's College but was unable to because she had Phyllis. So the legacy of Phyllis and Billy was deeply rooted in Falcon Pride. I always tell people that there are two things that Billy truly loves to talk about: his alma mater, St. Augustine's, and Alpha Phi Alpha Fraternity Incorporated.

It was Fall 1986, the roaring 20s for us. Billy had turned 20 in August, and I had turned 20 in November. That Fall, the Alphas were having a smoker. A smoker is an interest meeting to see if the fraternity is right for you.

Let's go back a little ways— oh, let's say before I was born. There was another fraternity that all my family members, cousins, and uncles were members of; heck, most of Johnston County were in this fraternity. Previously, I grew up with a Kappa paddle in my house and would pull it out from time to time to look at it. It was my Uncle Alfonso's paddle from when he pledged at Shaw University.My freshman year, all I hung around were Kappas and potential Kappas.

One of my mentors, who I sang in the Gospel Choir with and who was a Kappa, passed away from a heart attack in the summer of 1986. He was one of the first young people I had ever known to pass away so young. It affected me tremendously. It let me know that tomorrow is not promised for any of us. More on that later.

The Kappas would not roll out until Spring 1987, but the Alphas had a Fall 1986 line. After Tippy passed away, I started to research different fraternities. I saw that the Alphas were in all the leadership positions on campus. I saw the history of being the first of the first and the brothers who have impacted history in the African American community and the history of modern America after slavery. It was like a light bulb went off in my head. It was a no-brainer. This is who I am and who I would like to have a legacy with forever.

Curtis Thornton, Billy Lanier, Eric Thomas, Keven Wright, Lamont Hames, and Tony Pendleton were all at that smoker. There were seven of us. To Alpha, it's significant, being that there were seven founders.

Kenny Abrams and George McClamb left out due west, heading to Indiana for the Kappa train. The rest of us took that midnight train, and in jazz terminology, took the A Train north to the promised land.

Billy pledged Alpha because his sister Phyllis was an Alpha sweetheart and always talked about the guys in the fraternity. Billy looked up to these guys, and I knew that was what he wanted to be. Billy Lanier loves the black and old gold. In early December, we became Alpha men. Manly Deeds, Scholarship, and Love for all mankind are the aims of our dear fraternity.

Coach's Note:

God places people in your life exactly when you need them, even if you don't realize it yet.

THE COURT BECAME OUR CALLING

Billy worked at the Garner Road YMCA during his freshman and sophomore summers. He started coaching young men at the YMCA, and some of them went on to do big things. LeVelle Moton, now the head coach at North Carolina Central University, and Donald Williams from the 1992 National Championship team at the University of North Carolina at Chapel Hill were two who came out of the YMCA and went on to become great young men. This is where Billy got the itch to coach. The YMCA gave Billy an outlet to develop his coaching skills with the guidance of Ivan Chapman (our mentor and connector). Ivan had a connection with Cardinal Gibbons High School in Raleigh, NC, where the head coach, Jay Doherty, gave Billy an opportunity of a lifetime.

Billy and I could never be more grateful to Coach Doherty for allowing us to come in as young men and coach at one of the most prestigious high schools in the Raleigh area. We had some talented players at Cardinal Gibbons. One outstanding talent was Ronald Wilson, who went on to Villanova and won a Big East tournament championship playing for Coach Lappas. Coach Massimino was there before Coach Lappas; he recruited Ronald Wilson to Villanova and departed as the head coach. We also had a kid named Jeremy Harper, who was the first pure shooter I had ever seen besides Jimmy Batchelor and my cousin Wayne Ray. If we needed a basket, Coach Lanier would design a play for Jeremy in a heartbeat.

Billy was the junior varsity coach at the time and an assistant coach for the varsity program. I was an assistant to Billy on the JV team and an assistant on the varsity as well. We had one game that I remember oh so well. I think my brother Rod Watson, who coached at Potomac High School in Oxon Hill, MD, can relate.

We opened the season with the world-famous Oak Hill Academy out of Mouth of Wilson, Virginia. This team was ranked #1 in the nation. They had a player named Anthony Cage. We had a kid by the name of Abib, who was about 6'9", and Ronald Wilson, who was around 6'9" as well. The first play of the game was a tap to the guard for an alley-oop to Anthony Cage. Coach Doherty immediately called a timeout. This is how the season started for us at Cardinal Gibbons.

We learned a lot while at Cardinal Gibbons. We learned how to prepare game plans, exercise programs, and basketball organizational skills. We met many college coaches. During that time, Billy and I found our purpose in life.

One more quick story. We were coaching against Forsyth Day School in Winston-Salem for a JV championship game. Keith was at the free-throw line shooting a one-and-one when Billy called a timeout. I, being young and dumb, said, "Keith, man, you gotta make these shots." Billy looked at me with some communication skills that I recognized at the time to mean I should shut my mouth and said to Keith, "When you make these shots, we'll go on and win the game." That was the only time that I spoke before he did to a player. Billy's leadership skills were amazing at an early age. Thank you, Cardinal

Gibbons, for giving us the opportunity to begin what would go on to be a lifetime of coaching experience for a true legend of the game.

Coach's Note:

Surround yourself with culture, pride, and excellence. It will carry you through life.

THE 50-YARD LINE DREAM

Billy and Ivan coached AAU basketball. I really just stuck to the high school side of things, but from time to time, they would invite me to tournaments and to sit on the bench. I would also go and watch pickup games over at Gibbons and some of the high school talent AAU practices that took place.

There was a young man there who played like a grown man. This young man was from eastern North Carolina and would make his way to Raleigh to play with the AAU team. He played against grown men and dominated. He was given a visit to NC State during the NC State vs. Carolina football game. Billy, Ivan, the young man, and I were able to attend. This would be my first Carolina/NC State ball game. The visiting committee took the young man on a tour and let him meet some of the other players and coaches. Billy and I ended up on the 50-yard line. For us, we had reached the mountaintop in sports as we knew it at that time. That young man went on to another school to play and became a long-time player in the NBA. It showed us that hard work really pays off, and having a little luck can get you into some important rooms and spaces. Here we were, two country boys from right down the road, small towns, and on the 50-yard line of a

State/Carolina game. Not big for kids today, but it was pretty special for two country boys like us.

Coach's Note:

Fraternity is not about letters; it's about legacy, loyalty, and lifting each other up.

DEGREES, BROTHERHOOD, AND BECOMING

Remember that I stated earlier there were seven on my line who became the Alphas. Well, all seven of us graduated in the spring of '89. Some of us finished in four years, while others took an additional year. But for all seven, it was the perfect timing. Four live in the DMV, one in Richmond, VA, one in North Carolina, and one in the Midwest. I think Bill and I have seen all of them in the past five years. The brotherhood and kindred spirit we have for one another is truly amazing.

At that graduation, we took an iconic picture where we are all lined up as we would be in a pledge line, one through seven, with our diplomas in hand and smiles on our faces. Young men, looking forward to great things to come in the future, with high hopes, not knowing what the future would hold. The ups and downs that life has to bring, the families we would develop, the kids we would have, the memories we would cherish, and the greatness that will come from all seven great men.

There is nothing like an HBCU graduation, and I am so glad that I had a chance to experience one. Once again, I am so grateful to be a part of this legacy.

Coach's Note:

Graduation doesn't mean you've arrived.
It means you're just getting started.

NO MAP, JUST MOVES

From my sophomore year until after graduation, I worked for the Marriott Corporation. This was a great experience. I met so many people from all walks of life. I remember MC Lyte, Richard Petty, Bob Lanier, the UNLV basketball team, the Rolling Stones, the Leverts—you name it, the Crabtree Valley Marriott was the place to be and work. There were so many of us who worked there that attended local colleges in the area. It was like one big happy family. I was fortunate enough my senior year to be mentored by a young man named Bobby Vaughn. Bobby is the son of the legendary coach at Elizabeth City State University, Coach Vaughn. Bobby had played with Mark West, who played for the Phoenix Suns and Old Dominion University. Bobby was well established with Marriott, and I watched his every move.

At the end of summer into early fall, I was offered a position with the Marriott Corporation in Southfield, MI. The only thing I knew was that I was ready for the world. Without even knowing where Southfield, MI, was, I accepted the offer. In two weeks, I was in Southfield, MI, right outside of Detroit. I had family there and a couple of line brothers. I was in between Dearborn and Detroit, so there was a little flavor of both sides. I thought I was adapting to the area pretty well until winter came. In the South, when it snows, everything stops. In the North, when it snows, nothing stops. Lesson learned.

I had an issue with my immediate manager that I did not think was fair or just. I was being accused of something I did not do. I called my father, knowing his response. I elected not to call my mother, knowing her response. My father heard the frustration and feared for his son's life; these were his exact words: "Come on home, buddy." For him, it could have been for selfish reasons because he wanted me to join him at the funeral home. When my mom found out about my coming home, it was not a good thing.

As for Bill, he had moved in with Pete Leach (his high school best friend), and they taught together in Wake County. Pete went on to become a great football coach in the Wake County school system. The summer before I left, I would hang out with them all the time—playing Nintendo, going to parties, and just having a good old time. Bill was well-established as a teacher in Wake County schools.

True story: when I returned to North Carolina, one of the first places I stopped was Pete's and Bill's place. Pete had just told Billy, "Man, I sho' miss that Phil Mitchell." No sooner had Pete said that than I knocked on the door. They could not believe I was back from Michigan.

But to stay under Yvonne Mitchell's roof, who was already mad at my return, I had to get a job.

As I stated, Billy and Pete worked in the Wake County school system. I, however, was forced to choose a different path. I became known by my nickname from my freshman year in college: the insurance man. I ran a debit route in the southeast Raleigh neighborhoods. Chavis Heights was my debit route. I hooked up with a veteran agent by the name of Al.

Al introduced me to the game of golf. He told me that if I wanted to make big deals in insurance, I had to learn how to play golf. Al even took me to get my first set of golf clubs. After completing our debit runs, we would end up playing golf. I kept the clubs in the back of the car. Also, after debit runs, I would find myself in the afternoons over at Billy and Pete's apartment playing Nintendo. Pete even had a nickname for me. It seems like everywhere I go, people have a nickname for me. Every time Pete would see me coming up to the apartment, he would say, "Here comes big money." He would call me big money because I never appeared to be working—suit, tie, dress shoes, and always over at their house. Sometimes we would start playing Nintendo for hours, and it would be late at night. Our original plan was to go to the club. We were dressed and ready to go, but we kept playing game after game, not making it to the club, which probably saved our lives and definitely a lot of money.

Needless to say, the insurance gig did not last long. I was back at Yvonne's house looking for another job. Pete and Billy returned to the Wake County school system that fall. My mother stepped in for me and asked Mr. Clayton, who was a retired agriculture agent and then a teacher's aide at a local middle school, to find me a job. Thus, I ended up at Smithfield Elementary. I had to become PIC certified to work with the type of kids that no one else wanted to deal with. It was a great experience working with those kids. There was one young man that I mentored who was very smart but just needed guidance. To protect the young man, we'll just say that his name was "Joe." Joe was the reason that I received this job. No one wanted to work with Joe. I saw myself in Joe, and with that Mitchell spirit, I knew that I could reach him in some way. Joe's behavior improved, and his grades improved. He didn't destroy things like he used to. I was so proud of Joe. I even started working at the group home where Joe resided at night and on weekends.

Bill was working with the same type of kids in the Wake County school system and needed a summer job. He ended up working at the group home during the day. Billy has often shared with me some hilarious stories of kids trying to escape and run home after a field trip. It was rewarding but a tough job. You know, life doesn't always take you where you think you should be, but this journey that we were about to embark on was what God had for us.

That summer was also filled with fun and clubbing. Thursday night was Tremors; Friday night Tremors. We would give it a break on Saturday to maybe go out on a date with a nice young lady. Billy had his girlfriend at that time, who became his wife, and they hung out together a lot.

Quick story about that: it was All-Star weekend in Charlotte, NC. I had a buddy who said he had some tickets for us for the All-Star weekend. I called Billy, Billy's girlfriend, and Pete and told them to get ready. I was coming through, and we were headed to Charlotte. I got to the door and thought to myself, let me call my buddy just to confirm one last time that he had the tickets. Billy's girlfriend and Pete were packed and ready to go. Billy looked at Pete and his girlfriend and asked them where they were going. They said to him, "Why are you not packed?" Billy told them, "Phil ain't got no tickets." I knocked on the door and told them that I had to make a confirmation call. When I called my buddy, he could not hear me on the other end. So he asked, "Who is this again?" and I said, "This is Phil, man!" Billy looked at his girlfriend and Pete and said, "I told y'all so; Phil ain't had no tickets." I never lived that down. It was a lesson learned.

Coach's Note:

It's okay to leave. It's okay to come home. What matters is that you keep moving forward.

SUMMERTIME MEMORIES
ON A TIGHT BUDGET

The summer before we moved to Washington, DC, we took a couple of trips, one being to Miami, FL, where the Alpha Phi Alpha National Convention was being held. Billy and I decided to drive from North Carolina to Miami. We got in the car and drove from North Carolina to the Florida state line. Road trips and road trip music were our thing. We got to the top of Florida and said, "Wow, we made it to Florida," not knowing that we had another 400 miles to go. This was the longest trip that we had ever driven, but we felt so free and young.

We got down to Miami and stayed at the Howard Johnson Motel. We explained that we wanted to stay two nights at the hotel. The front desk staff must have misunderstood what I was trying to explain to them. By 12:00 o'clock, they were calling the room, asking us if we wanted to stay another night. We explained to them that we had paid for two nights, we thought. They said, "No, you only paid for one night." Billy and I immediately gathered our things and went to another Howard Johnson Motel.

I had family in Miami at the time. Milton Price and Matthew Price lived in Miami and were very hospitable during the weekend.

We toured Biscayne Bay, met some of the Bee Gees on a jet ski, and saw Miami and its mansions and everything it had to offer. We also attended a couple of Alpha functions and met some outstanding brothers. It is amazing how much we enjoyed ourselves right out of college with so little money. A trip like that today would cost you well over $2,000.

Later that summer, we took another trip to visit friends in Atlanta, GA. I had moved them to Atlanta earlier in the summer. We rented a car, and again, my cousin Milton was with us. Here we go, rolling down 85 to Hotlanta. I had rented a car, and we had spent most of our money that Friday night, and we still had Saturday and Sunday to be in Atlanta. The young ladies that we were visiting were more like family—Delta sisters from North Carolina Central University. One I had known since high school, and the other we had known since college. Milton had attended North Carolina Central University as well. As I stated before, we were running low on cash— nothing new to us. We wanted to eat out but were again short on cash. We saw an Applebee's and knew we could afford to buy the girls at least some lunch. Billy said, "Let's pull on in there and eat." My cousin Milton then stated, "Man, we're in Atlanta; we just don't want to eat at any old eatery." Billy looked at me. I looked at Billy, and Billy said, "Man, if you don't pull this car into the Applebee's." Laughter filled the car because that was the type of friends we had.

Later that evening, we went out to the Dominique Wilkins club. We were in line when Dominique came out. He was selecting people to go in. There were two nice-looking sisters in front of us. Our friends were behind us, so it looked like we were a group. Dominique looked at the two girls and at us and said, "Everybody gets in." We were overjoyed. We had a great time in Atlanta that weekend, again always going places with little to no money.

We returned to Raleigh, and back to work we went. Summer fun is always good, but when you do it with family and great friends, those are memories of a lifetime.

Coach's Note:

You don't need much to have a good time— just a little gas money, a lot of laughter, and real friends.

8

THE CALL THAT CHANGED EVERYTHING

After the summer fun was over, I was still working at the Rainbow House, and Bill was getting ready to return to the Wake County Public School System. It was late July/early August when we got a phone call—a phone call that would change our lives forever. You see, I had been laid off by the Johnston County Public School due to a budget crunch for new hires. At the time, the Superintendent was my old principal from high school. I remember him coming into the school and announcing that there would be budget cuts at a teachers' meeting. You know how the old saying goes: last hired, first fired.

So that call came right on time. Remember, there were no cell phones, only landlines. On the other end of that phone call was Rod Watson. He knew that I was working at Smithfield Elementary. Rod was working as a teacher in the Prince George's County school system. Rod called me and said, "Hey bro, they are hiring black males to teach in Prince George's County." Without hesitation, I immediately said, "I'll be there in a couple of days." Without hesitation again, I immediately called Billy. Within a couple of days, Billy and I were traveling to Maryland to sign our teaching contracts. Mr. Ed Holes and Robert Gaskins were waiting for us at the Central Office in Upper Marlboro, MD. They welcomed us with open arms. It felt like home. We left Maryland, returned to North Carolina, got our things out of storage, and loaded up a U-Haul, never looking back. Within a week's time, we were back in Prince George's County, Maryland.

My mom's family lived in the DMV, so I spent many summers and holidays in the area. In fact, the school that I was assigned to was one where my Uncle Alphonso had previously taught, and my cousin Elsie Wiggs had previously worked with Mr. Gaskins.

Billy was assigned to Robert Goddard Middle School with Rod. Bill taught Special Education classes and was a great fit for the school. Bill and Rod would end up coaching the Robert Goddard basketball team. I, along with Ric Huguley, would coach the Francis Scott Key Middle School team. I think we played them twice; they won one game, and we won one game. Most of their players came from Landover and Greenbelt, MD. Most of our players came from Capitol Heights, Suitland, and the Silver Hill Rd. area. We had some outstanding players and all-around good kids.

We had stepped into a future that we could only imagine back in North Carolina. To us, Prince George's County was our saving grace.

Coach's Note:

Sometimes, your breakthrough is just one phone call and one yes away.

9

LIVING THE LIFE

When we moved to Maryland, we forgot one thing: where in the world were we going to stay? Rod said that we could stay with him in his one-bedroom apartment. I think we lasted all but two months before we moved. We had saved up a couple of checks and moved to Burtonsville, MD, where we linked up with a couple of line brothers and another Alpha brother that we knew.

The apartment we had would cost about $3500 to live in today. We were fortunate to get the place for about $900. I had my own walk-in closet, a bathroom with a full shower, and a room that could fit a queen-size bed. There was a huge living room and a country kitchen with a balcony off the kitchen. Bill was way back in the back bedroom with the same amenities as my room. We were living the life. We taught, worked at after-school programs, and went to happy hours on Fridays in Greenbelt, MD. Then we would run the streets of Georgetown and DC until about 2:00 or 3:00 in the morning. Life was good. My cousin Milton even moved up from Miami and lived in Maryland for a couple of years.

The kids we taught were a little different. I remember when Bill came home one day and fell asleep on the couch. I was sitting there watching the news in the living room when Bill started talking in his sleep. Let's just say the kid's name was "James." Billy was talking in his sleep and said, "James, we only got 5 minutes. Can you just stay still for 5 minutes, and you'll be outta here?"

I fell out laughing, and when Billy woke up, I said to him, "This James kid must be really working your nerves at school." He asked me how I knew about James. I told him that he kept mentioning him in his sleep. Both of us just fell out laughing.

In that same apartment, in that same living room, we learned the shocking news that Magic Johnson, Bill's favorite basketball player of all time, had contracted the AIDS virus. I will never forget the look on Billy's face when he heard that. It was almost like someone had passed away at that moment. There's also another story about the Lakers. I had a buddy who played for them in the early '90s, and I had obtained the Lakers organization's phone number. So I called the Great Western Forum. Billy didn't believe me, so I let him hear the conversation. Ring, ring. The lady picked up and said, "The Great Western Forum." I said, "No way." The lady replied, "Yes way." I went on to ask if I could leave a message or talk to that friend of mine. She said, "One second, please." The next lady picked up and said, "LA Lakers." Again, I said, "No way." The lady then said, "Yes way." Billy had a fit, and seeing the joy on his face knowing that I was talking to someone in the Lakers organization was just a joy for him. I left a message for my buddy, but he never called me back. But it's just a simple fact that we were able to communicate with Billy's favorite basketball organization.

Life in Burtonsville was great. We were only there for two years, but it was wonderful to be under 25 and living in the DMV.

Coach's Note:

*Choose your roommates wisely; sometimes,
they become your family.*

10

WE IS MARRIED NOW

Life has its ways of putting people in your space that cannot change. Throughout this book, you will see that this guy was a Godsend to me. But right around the corner from where we lived, God brought someone else back into my life. This young lady asked me to marry her when the time was right. We started talking again and eventually made it official in the summer of 1992. This meant that Bill and I would be separated once again, but only by marriage. This meant that playtime was over as far as running the streets. It was time to get serious about life and taking on a wife.

Bill and I eventually moved away from Burtonsville. I moved in with my aunt Annie Lou and her husband Uncle Lonnie to save up for the wedding the next year. Bill found a place in Laurel, MD, for a couple of months.

Bill was dating his college sweetheart at the time and was going back and forth to North Carolina. We were at an event at Bowie State University. This event was for black male achievers, headed up by Robert Gaskins. There were so many brothers there that it made you feel proud to be a black male. There was a young man there who needed a roommate. Somehow, Mr. Gaskins mentioned that I had moved out and that if anybody was looking for a roommate, they should get in touch with Bill Lanier. There was a young social studies teacher, Theo Cramer, who would go on to do great things in Prince George's County and the surrounding school systems here in the great state of Maryland. He was from the South, like Bill and myself, and was ready to help kids achieve in life. This was a program for young men to get a master's degree at Bowie State University. Billy, Cramer, and eventually our line brother Lamont became roommates. The choices we make can sometimes come back to haunt us. Theo and Lamont went on to Bowie State and received a master's degree. Billy and I started but did not finish because we wanted to coach. I think we lasted one semester or two. We went on to Trinity College to earn master's credits without finishing the master's degree—lots of credit but no degree. Young people, get all the education, certificates, and knowledge you can about a particular topic before life happens.

In the summer of 1993, I was married and moving on as a husband. Bill was living with Theo and Lamont, and was single at the time. As the old saying goes, "monkey see, monkey do." Bill and his college sweetheart were right behind us and getting married. Bill had a beautiful wedding on the campus of St. Augustine's College at the chapel. Now comes the saying... "We *is* married now!!!"

Coach's Note:

Marriage is not the end of the brotherhood. It just adds more people to love.

11
____

CAROLINA BLUE

In the summer of 1993, Bill ran into a frat brother at a church in Southeast Washington, DC. The brother was coaching at Eastern High School on Capitol Hill in Washington, DC. We had met the brother at an Alpha function years ago. You see, God already knows who is gonna be in your life as long as you live your life. Hold on to that one for a little later.

Coach William Chiselom went to Livingstone with my brother Ernest Cooley, his wife/my sister Delina, and a brother that I met in college, Eric Norman. Coach Chisholm asked Billy if he knew of anyone who would like to coach football. Bill eventually mentioned my name. We invited Coach Chisholm over to our house in Silver Spring, MD. There, we broke bread together and talked about college days. It was Billy making connections for a brother once again. I think you kinda get the theme of this book. There is no me without him, and there is no him without me.

Once the dinner was over, I had a job as an assistant football coach at Eastern High School. Coach Chisholm eventually became the head coach, and he offered me the head JV coach position. The

JV team went on to win a couple of JV Championships during my tenure.

Right after the first season at Eastern High School for football, Coach Mark Hurt offered Billy the JV basketball job at Roosevelt High School in Greenbelt, MD. Coach Hurt then asked Billy if he knew of someone who would want to coach with them. Once again, Billy called on me. It was Coach Mark Hurt, Billy, myself, and Coach Glenn Farello, head coach at Paul VI Catholic High School in Chantilly, VA. Roosevelt High School's basketball program needed to be revived, and Coach Mark Hurt brought that program back to life. As you can see,  these coaches—Coach William Chiselom, Coach Mark Hurt, and Coach Jay Doherty—gave us the opportunity to grow.

After Coach Mark Hurt moved out of state, Coach Farello took over and made the program even greater. You now see the great things and the great players that he has coached at Paul VI. Thank you, Roosevelt, for letting us be a part of something great. Oh yeah, both Eastern High School and Roosevelt High School had the Carolina Blue uniforms. Destiny.

Coach's Note:

Coaching is a calling. You may be the only father figure some of these kids ever see.

12

BUILDING LEGACY, BRICK BY BRICK

Last season at Roosevelt, we played a team from southern Prince George's County. The team was the Roosevelt of the southern portion of the county. They had an outstanding player by the name of Dwayne Moore. Dwayne spoke to us in the stands before his game. He was a senior at Oxon Hill High School. I still remember what Dwayne said at the end of our conversation. The young man looked at us and said, "I wish you guys were at Oxon Hill." Out of the mouths of babes comes good fortune.

At the end of the season, there was an opportunity to head to the southern portion of the county. Billy applied for and received the job at Oxon Hill.

The school colors are significant in this situation—black and gold. There was no question that this was the place to be. When Billy told me that he was hired as the coach at Oxon Hill, he indicated that we just got the job at Oxon Hill. The joy that I saw on Billy's face was something I had never seen before. Not even at graduation from St. Augustine College had I seen that face.

We immediately hit the ground running. We sat in the gym, the aircraft carrier, just him and me, thinking about the endless possibilities of beginning a great program for this beautiful and outstanding community. As we were sitting there, excited about what was going to happen, in walked a young man who would ultimately be our saving grace: Lamar Butler (hometown legend). He had a deep relationship to the community like no other. He was a D.C. legend, a Bowie State legend, and had tried out for some NBA teams.

It would be the three of us and another young coach by the name of Coach Fells.

Our first season, we went 5-15. As the old ball coaches say... not very good. But with the presence of Coach Butler and Coach Lanier at the Oxon Hill Boys' and Girls' Club almost every Saturday after our practice, the players started to matriculate to the high school program. We were building from the ground up. We fundraised, and we had the best parents in the world, and the community got involved. There is one incident that took place which brought the community, the school, and the team together. It was right before Christmas break when a young man by the name of Chucky was shot at the bus stop on the school campus. Coach Lanier had implemented a study hall where the JV and Varsity would be together for their studies. This way, we had an account of all our players, and we were building young men for college-bound students. I remember Coach Lanier talking to the players about what had just happened. It would make anybody want to get far away from that school and community. But Coach Lanier went on and had practice anyway. Not knowing the outcome for the young man, Coach Lanier pulled everybody together at center court, thus beginning an Oxon Hill tradition. He told us that the young man, Chucky, had passed, but he also comforted everyone in that circle. He let the players and managers know that the coaches were not going anywhere. That is how you build a foundation for something that becomes an everlasting legacy.

I was told by a professional football player that Oxon Hill had a good run while our coaching staff was there. I tend to agree with the old fellow who has the Super Bowl ring.

It was an outstanding display of how a program should be run. From Little League to Major Leagues, from Pee Wee to the NFL, from Oxon Hill to the NBA, we set an example, starting with Coach Lanier's leadership.

During the summers, we started a JV league at Oxon Hill. This included teams from Northern Virginia and from points south of Central Ave. It was a very competitive league. It actually made all the programs better, and the fellowship with the coaches was second to none. Coach Butler provided us with jerseys and all our gear—sweatsuits, caps, hoodies—anything we needed as far as apparel, Coach Butler was the man.

The name of the league was the LBM Summer League. This league allowed kids to develop their basketball skills during the summer, which made them better for the upcoming season. We ran the league for about five years, giving way to participating in other leagues that had developed for JV players.

Our second year at Oxon was a major improvement. I think we went 15-5, improving and getting better with every game.

Year 3 was even better than Year 2. We added new coaches, Lamar Barrett and Kevin Smack. They were outstanding young men and HBCU-groomed. I will never forget how excited Billy was when these two guys were added to the coaching staff. The family was growing.

I want to share a story about our first major recruit and home visit. It was around 1996, and Terrence Nixon was being recruited by George Mason. At that time, Paul Westhead, former coach of the Lakers, was the coach at George Mason. Coach Westhead was at the table with myself, Billy, Terrence, and Terrence's mother. Coach Westhead was giving his spiel about the program, but all I saw was that Lakers championship ring on his hand. Being a Lakers fan, I'm sure Billy didn't miss it either. By the end of the recruiting visit, I think everyone at the table was leaning towards George Mason. Unfortunately and fortunately, Coach Westhead moved on from George Mason, and in walked Jim Larrañaga. Coach Larrañaga had an immediate impact on the George Mason program. We will talk more about that later.

Coach's Note:

Success comes when discipline, love, and belief meet at center court.

VICTORY, LOSS, AND LEGACY

The 1997-1998 season was like a coming-out party. No one had given us a chance to do what we would do that year. We added another coach to the staff by the name of John Gonsalves. Coach Gonsalves was a former college player at Northeastern University in Massachusetts. He was an outstanding student of the game of basketball. So now we had the dream team of coaches, some very young athletes combined with some savvy veterans to compete and make some noise.

This was an emotional time for me personally as I was continuing to battle with the fact that my father had been diagnosed with prostate cancer. The doctor told my mother and me that my dad only had a short time to live in 1995. My dad battled through prostate cancer for three years.

Back to the season, we won some games that we were not supposed to win, and by this time, everybody in the county had taken notice. Gyms were packed, and our band and cheerleaders were the best in the county. We had the best athletic director ever, Ms. Christine Johnson. Our principal, Dr. David Stofa, and vice principals were all supportive of what we were trying to do. Everything fell into place that year. We reached the Regional Championship and won. Now we were on to Cole Field House on the University of Maryland's campus. The week before the semifinal game, my dad broke his hip. My mom needed my help. So, as I had done for the past three years every other weekend, I went to North Carolina to attend to my father and help my mother. The Thursday night game was against Mervo Technical High School out of Baltimore—a tough team, as most Baltimore teams are—but they ran into a buzz saw that night. I received a call from Billy indicating that we had won. My dad and mom were excited, and they saw that I wanted to be there. My dad looked at me and said, "Go ahead on back, buddy. I will be fine." That Saturday morning before the championship game, I got on the road and headed back to Maryland. I dropped off my clothes at home and headed over to Cole Field House. I got there before the team arrived and was in the locker room setting up.

Just to walk out and see those names in the rafters and reflect on the history of events that had taken place in that building—one being that the first all-black starting lineup team beat the mighty Kentucky team, coached by Adolf Rupp, some 30 years ago before this night. You start to feel a certain kind of way. The team arrived, focused as always—no talking on the bus on the way to the games; a big Billy rule. The guys acted like they had been there before. It was a proud moment for the Oxon Hill Community.

As Billy and I sat there on the bench before the game, he asked for his gum, and I provided him with a piece. I said to him, "You know, Billy, this is big time for two small-town country boys like ourselves." Then I said this: "You know Michael Jordan dunked in that very goal," and began pointing to the goal. Billy looked at me with his eyes wide open. He later told me that, at that moment, he had butterflies in his stomach.

I know that many participants in that game would like me to stop talking about the game against Gaithersburg in the 1998 state championship, but it was a moment for the entire county. It was a moment for Coach Billy Lanier. It was a moment for the DMV. It was a record that still stands today—the longest state championship game in Maryland history.

You're always questioning yourself: should we have done this or should we have done that? But we cannot second-guess ourselves in the game of life. All of our steps are ordered, and in that game, all of the kids laid their hearts on the line. Later on, in June of 1998, Billy, Lamar Barrett, and I had the opportunity to work at the John Thompson Basketball Camp. This was one of the bucket list events of my life. We worked the camp for two weeks under the tutelage of Coach Thompson, teaching drills and coaching campers from around the world. Billy and I roomed together and were across the hall from two players that you may know: Joakim Noah and Little Patrick.

Quick story: Little Patrick was reading an ESPN magazine in the hallway as I was approaching the room. There was a picture of his father with the "Got Milk" ad on the back cover. I had one of those moments where the son is reading a magazine, and his father is on the back cover in an ad. It was such an exciting moment. It was unbelievable, and I immediately became a fan. That was a high moment. I later experienced one of my lowest moments. As soon as I got home and was preparing to go to North Carolina for a family reunion, I received a call from my cousin Steve indicating that my father had passed. My mother saw him the day before he passed. At that moment, she said to him, "Philip, be good now." He replied, "Yvonne, I will be as good as I can." He left us on July 3, 1998. I went from a high moment to one of my lowest in a span of 24 hours. God never makes mistakes. Rest in peace, Dad.

In 1999, we made it back to the state championship game, losing at the buzzer to Southern Baltimore.

Coach's Note:

Big moments don't come with instructions. You show up. You give your all. That's enough.

14

THE SHOW, THE RINGS, THE TROPHY

In 1999, the summer and fall preseason had begun, with lots of anticipation to close the deal on the state championship. The young fellas who played in the longest overtime game in Maryland state history are now seniors and looking to close the deal on a state championship.

We were ranked in the Washington Post in the top 10 for three years. In the summer of 1999, we participated in the Georgetown Oxon Kenner League championship game and won against our archrival Roosevelt High School. In that game were several future NBA players: Eddie Basden, Delonte West, and Michael Sweetney. The starting lineup consisted of a Final Four player, Lamar Butler Jr.; Phil Goss, who played for Drexel University; and a player who later played at DePaul, Delonte Holland, from Roosevelt High School. The level of talent on that floor that day was amazing. The gym was packed, and Coach John Thompson was in attendance. Oxon Hill and Roosevelt always battled, and the games always went down to the wire because we knew each other so well. By winning this summer league, it propelled us into a top-ranked team in the area. You're talking about some of the most outstanding high school basketball in the country: DeMatha, Gonzaga, Roosevelt, Dunbar of Washington, D.C., Archbishop Carroll, and of course the mighty Clippers of Oxon Hill. The vision and the goal were in front of us. All we had to do was work hard, not be selfish, love, and play together.

Our season went as planned, winning the regional championship and moving on to the states.We reached the championship game, but this time it was against Quince Orchard High School of Montgomery County. Unlike 1998, we were determined to close the deal. And that is what we did. I was so happy for that coaching staff, our athletic director, Ms. Christine Johnson, our principal, Ron Curtis, and the entire administrative team. Without their support, this would have never been possible. Oh yeah, Billy's mom came to the game and saw her son win a state championship. There is nothing more precious than a mom seeing her son accomplish such a phenomenal feat. It wouldn't be the last time Coach Lanier would reach the championship game for the State of Maryland.

Coach's Note:

Winning is sweet. But doing it the right way—
that's legendary.

15

FROM BUZZERS TO BOTTLES

You should see a pattern by now as we follow this story called life. During this season, I guess the heat didn't work in the house of Billy and me.

Around October and December of the year 2000, two children were born. Billy had a little girl, and as for me, a little boy. I had accepted a job at John Philip Sousa Middle School in Washington, D.C. So for me at that time, basketball had taken a back seat. Baby and family first was the order of the day.

Bill and his staff continued to coach at Oxon Hill for a few more years, winning another state championship in 2004. Folks, can you say outstanding career? They even built a new gym for the old Clippers. I hope someday that the school can find it in their heart to at least name the floor after Billy Lanier. In December of 2001, my mother passed. Once again, Billy was there to help me through that tough time, along with my extended family, and I was able to make it through.

At the end of the month, the Oxon Hill Clippers were invited to a tournament in Delaware. At this tournament were LeBron James and JJ Redick. The Clippers got a chance to play against JJ Redick and beat his team at the buzzer. I met the team there and took my son, who was only one year old. That night, we witnessed, arguably, one of the top 10 players ever to play the game, LeBron James. For me, I will always be a Jordan fan. But having my son sitting at center court floor seats watching LeBron James play was priceless. I often tease my son that he fell asleep on LeBron James. I will give him a break because he was only one year old, and Daddy had him running around all day long. To be in the King's presence at that time was an amazing feeling.

For me, I was starting to think differently and move differently regarding my future. It was more about family than basketball. Although we would attend Final Fours and have fun with the coaches we had developed friendships with from all over the United States, it was so wonderful to be recognized in that space.

One quick story about Billy: We were in Minnesota for the Final Four with the Maryland Terps. We were leaving Minnesota and were at the airport when a young fella from California came up to Billy and said to him, "Hey, you're Coach Lanier." And Billy said, "Yes, I am." The young man asked, "Would you guys come out to California and play in a tournament?" Because of the Dunbar rule, we were unable to go. If you're not familiar with the Dunbar rule, look it up and think of Muggsy Bogues, David Wingate, and Reggie Lewis. That should give you the answer right there. That is how recognized the Oxon Hill program was in the United States at that time. Nowadays, people recognize Oxon Hill as the National Harbor.

Coach's Note:

Your biggest legacy won't be trophies.
It'll be your children.

16

FROM THE SIDELINE TO STATE LINES

As Bill continued to coach and work in the DMV, my wife and I, at the time, were looking for something different. We had welcomed a baby girl into the family. There is nothing like kids to make you feel proud. My two kids and Billy's daughter are our hearts.

With that said, my wife and I, at the time, dropped everything, sold the house, and moved to Pennsylvania. It would be the first time that Billy and I would be apart since I took the job in Michigan. The year was 2004, and Billy had just won his second state championship. I think we kind of caught folks off guard when we said we were moving to Pennsylvania. I don't know if Billy was prepared for me leaving. He often called me. That's when life got a little strange for him. I was kind of the one who would bring him back into reality, and he had grown accustomed to me being there. Folks, we all need each other.

Just before the move, though, was a high moment for the community of Oxon Hill, Prince George's County, and the state of Maryland when Michael Sweetney, who attended Georgetown, became a lottery pick for the New York Knicks. Oh, what joy it was during that time. Life can bring you highs and lows. That June was a high point, but life can also bring the low points in a matter of months, days, and weeks. For the Sweetney family, it would not be long before the head of the household would pass away. A member of our Oxon Hill family was lost, and we were all devastated.

Our move to Pennsylvania was a difficult yet rewarding one, as well. Since my parents had both passed away at the time, it was nice to be around my in-laws. The kids were one and three years old, and in preschool and kindergarten.

Before I moved, I went into the office of Mr. Lipscomb, the principal at Sousa, and told him that I was leaving to move to Pennsylvania. Mr. Lipscomb looked at me and said these direct words: "Do you even have a job in Pennsylvania?" I looked at him and said, "No, sir." The look of horror on his face when I told him that! As the move took place, I could not get his words out of my head when my salary was cut in half as a result of that move to Pennsylvania. Pennsylvania had its ups and its downs.

After three years, we moved back to Maryland. Felix and Oscar were back together again.

Quick story: during the summer of 2006, I was still in Pennsylvania, and our fraternity had the National Convention in Washington, D.C. Actually, it was the 100th anniversary of the fraternity. So, this was Billy's and my second National Convention that we attended.

At that time, I was driving the BMW, and Billy and I had the sunroof open, Bose speakers playing jazz, smoking a couple of cigars, and enjoying life. We stopped at a stoplight and both got quiet. He looked at me, and I looked at him, and I knew that I had to get back to Maryland.

Brotherhood— we all need that one person to have our backs through the good and the bad. I was there when his mother transitioned during that same time. All of you know that there's something about losing a mother that will never be replaced. I think at that point, my mind said I had to get back to Maryland one way or the other.

Coach's Note:

Don't be afraid to start over.
God never wastes obedience.

17

HOME DIDN'T FEEL LIKE HOME

In 2007, we made the transition back to Maryland. My wife at the time indicated that she had a job in Maryland and that we should move back. In less than a week, we had the truck packed up and were on our way back to Maryland, this time settling in Columbia, MD.

This was an excellent choice for the kids and the school system that Howard County provided. In 1998, when we lived in Laurel, MD, and helped raise our niece, Marines, Laurel High School was much like the schools of Howard County. My niece went on to become a University of Maryland graduate and later earned her master's degree, as well. She was my first daughter and has been a great role model, along with her husband, for my kids. It takes a village.

Howard County was very different for me. Somewhere along the way, I had lost confidence in myself. I was dealing with a lot of depressed thoughts and a lack of confidence in the person I was before I left Maryland. I was very protective of my spirit and became somewhat hard and reserved. My trust in people had been eroded. I think I still have some residue today. On the outside, I can make anybody laugh and feel like they are their best. I had moved away from my Lord and Savior and had tried to do life by myself.

At that point, Coach Lanier was a very popular guy. Since I was away, he found a new set of friends. They were great guys to hang around with and very successful. They loved Coach more than he ever knew. Those guys are still around today, making sure that Coach has everything he needs.

As I returned to Maryland, I went to a very low place. At the time, I didn't want family or friends to know that life had taken a turn for the worse. I was working at night and teaching in Prince George's County during the day.

I had become a shell of myself. My relationship with my then-wife wasn't good, and I was making it worse. I felt like just running away from it all. And eventually, I did.

A lot of people don't understand it, but as the kids say today – it is what it is. We don't realize when we go through stuff that it affects everyone around us. I can say in my circle that there are more divorced people than there are married people. That's a sad statement.

We let the lease run out, and I filed for divorce. The person who kind of picked me up and was there for me in my darkest hour was, you guessed it, Coach Billy Lanier. I may not have seen him every day, but it was about three times a week. The man told me to hang in there. He knew that there were times when I was sleeping in my truck. Brotherhood and friendship are so important. He even contacted someone to get me a job that helped me get back on my feet and propelled me back into the game of life. I could have been dead and gone, but he saw fit to help me at my lowest point. If there's any lesson I learned during this time, it is that we should not suffer in silence.

He even took me to First Baptist Church of Glenarden a couple of times. This fed my spirit until I was able to find my church home, Celebration Church at Columbia, where I still attend today. That was 2009. I thank God for the journey. I thank God for Billy Lanier.

I crossed back over the Mason-Dixon Line thinking I was coming home. What I didn't know was that my brother was the bridge.

Coach's Note:

Never suffer in silence. Your healing starts when you ask for help.

18

WALKING OFF THE COURT
FOR THE LAST TIME

Around 2013-2014, Bill had an opportunity to go back to Oxon Hill to coach again. I think we were sitting at the Starbucks in Largo, MD, when Bill asked me to come coach again at Oxon Hill. I was so excited and immediately said yes. The last time I had worked with Bill was at Flowers High School, but that was short-lived due to starting a new job and transportation issues at the time.

I had not coached in the new gym, so this was all new to me. It was a very different experience this time around, though. I had been sick and was going through health challenges even at that time. My focus had changed, and Bill's focus had changed, as well. It felt like time had passed us by. We added Coach Walker and Coach Fraiser, and we tried to reinvent something that had given us so much joy.

The season was almost like our first season at Oxon Hill, where we started out slow. Our last game that we coached together was at Bowie High School in Bowie, MD. Bowie had a pretty good team that year, and we were at the bottom of the county. Bill was frustrated with how the season went; his focus was somewhere else, not just on basketball.

At the end of the season, we took some time off. Two weeks later, we went to a golf tournament in Bethesda. Around the 9th hole, Billy pulled me off to the side, and I asked him when we were starting offseason training. Billy looked at me with a blank face and said that he would not be returning as the head coach at Oxon Hill. I was so disappointed, but I understood that look. By him telling me, it seemed like it was a relief and that he could move on with his life. I never questioned it again because I knew that this chapter in our lives was over.

Also, my son was playing basketball and was pretty good, so I wanted to follow him on his journey, and that's what I did. Bill stayed away from attending my son's games. He only came to one AAU game where my son hit the winning shot. Billy told him after the game, "Monte, that was a bad shot." Monte said to him, "Uncle Billy, I made the shot." We all laughed.

Although we only went back for one year at Oxon Hill, it provided us closure to one of the greatest chapters in our lives. Through this book, I hope to advocate for Billy A. Lanier and encourage others in the basketball community to consider him for induction into the Maryland Basketball Hall of Fame.

Coach's Note:

When a chapter closes with love and respect, there's nothing left to regret.

19

MY BROTHER'S KEEPER...
MY ASSIGNMENT

At the end of 2019, things started to go left. In November of 2019, we lost our dear brother Kevin Smack. Not long after that, Ms. Johnson, our dear athletic director, lost her daughter. Billy and I were devastated.

In January 2020, we lost one of the greatest ballplayers of all time —Kobe Bryant. His daughter Gigi was with him and passed as well. This really affected Billy in ways that we would not understand at that time.

In March 2020, Billy and I were watching the last game that the Maryland Terps would play that year. COVID-19 would send us into isolation for the rest of the year. I did not see Bill from March 2020 through December 2020. We would call and check in on each other to see how we were making it through the pandemic. He sounded good and was always asking me how I was doing.

It was not until May 2021 that I saw him again. Billy's birthday is in August, along with his sister Phyllis. Billy posted a picture of him and Phyllis during their birthday. The post indicated that Phyllis had completed her cancer treatment and everything was good. I was praising the Lord that my sister had completed treatment and was doing fine.

That October, I was back in the hospital with shortness of breath and swollen legs. I had to be on oxygen during that time. The doctors were able to get the swelling down, and I returned home. It's something how fast life can change—one day you're up, and the next you're almost dead.

In mid-November, I received a call indicating that Billy was in the hospital and that he had a stroke. With COVID-19 restrictions, I wasn't able to get to my brother. In the next two weeks, life for Billy would forever change. His dear beloved sister Phyllis passed away while he was in the hospital. Billy went from bad to worse as far as the stroke.

Fast forward to late December 2020; still having breathing problems and swelling in my feet, my daughter came to see me. With sadness, she looked at me and said, "Daddy, you have to go to the hospital." I could not walk from the living room to the kitchen and back to the den without getting out of breath. So, I told her to bring me some food, and I would go after I ate. She took me to the hospital, and after a few tests, they determined that I had kidney failure. I was immediately rushed into surgery and started the process of going on dialysis. As I stated in the beginning and in the title of this book, *we have done life together*.

I started on dialysis, and Billy was in a rehab center. Both of us were sick and in need of the help of others. I had a team of people who are still in my circle today. You know who you are and what you did for me, and I am eternally grateful still to this day. Billy's team was strong as well. I know without a doubt that he appreciates everyone and would love to articulate that to you.

In April 2021, frat brother Keven Wright and I made a visit to see Billy at the rehab facility. Billy was sitting there, and when we walked in, he was overjoyed with tears. We laughed, cried, and laughed some more. It was a good visit. We returned a couple more times to see him, but it was the last time we visited that really tore me up inside. I had never heard a man cry like that before, where it was coming from so deep inside. It was a cry for help, and Keven and I felt that. In order to get Billy to stop crying, out of the blue, I said, "We're gonna get you out of here, and let's pray about it right now." Keven offered a prayer, and Billy's spirit calmed down. What a mighty God we serve! We often say that God is not the author of confusion, and in that moment, peace came.

As Keven and I were traveling back to my place, we talked about it. Knowing me all of my adult life, Keven understood that my mind was made up. I was not going to change my mind, and I was going to get Billy out of that place. It took about a month after that for us to schedule a meeting. I was still going through dialysis, but as my cousin Steve told me, my situation was just a lifestyle change. With that confirmation from my older brother, I knew that I could be strong for both of us. Have I had moments of doubt? Yes, I'm only human. Has it been tough? When you're Felix and Oscar (some of you will get that later), yes, it has. But it has been well worth it!

During this journey, Billy has lost a lot. His father, his uncle, and his favorite cousin also went on to glory during this difficult time. He was out of rehab and was able to attend his father's and cousin's funerals and find closure during a challenging time.

No one knows what the future holds for us. We only have today. I would not change anything about my life's journey. A good brother from another mother gave me a compliment. He said, "Man, it is amazing what you're doing for Billy." I looked the brother in the eye and said, "At this point in time, my brother, it is my assignment." You see, we have to know what our assignments are when God calls them to our attention. Doing what I did probably saved both of our lives by being obedient to my heart and what God was saying to me at the time: to take care of my brother in his darkest hour; to not fear the future of death; to move forward even when it's tough; and to think of others before thinking of yourself.

You see, on February 20, 2022, I received a gift of life– a donated kidney. Although it gave me life, it was a gift that nobody wanted. There were some diseases in the kidney that would frighten the average person. Trusting in God, I said to my team at the hospital, "I will take it." They assured me the diseases were curable. What kind of person would I have been to turn my nose up at God's gift of life? Because it was Steve who said it best – it was just a lifestyle change.

All of my monthly reports have been satisfactory or above. The diseases that the kidney could potentially produce have all been treated and are no more. The kidney is functioning well. I would like to thank all the doctors and the medical team that has helped us during this difficult journey. I will end by saying this: Am I my brother's keeper? My reply is, YES, I AM!

Coach's Note:

God gave me the strength to walk through the fire– not just for me, but for my brother.

ACKNOWLEDGMENTS

First and foremost, I give thanks to God — the true Head of my life, even in the seasons when I did not put HIM first. Thank You, Lord, for this life's journey. There were many times I wish I had listened to YOU instead of trying to do things my own way. Yet You never left me. I love You more and more each day.

To my family on both sides — my mom's folks and my dad's folks — I am truly a better MAN because of you. Your love for me is unmatched. That agape love. The kind of love that surpasses all understanding. Thank you for shaping me, supporting me, and standing by me.

To my children — Marines, my bonus child, thank you for sharing the original vision for the book cover. Olivia, thank you for helping write my author bio. And last but certainly not least, my number one son, Monte, thank you for your unwavering support. It is because of you three that I am still here. You gave me something to live for when I needed it most. I am so proud of the adults you have become. I want you to know that as long as I have breath in my body, you are deeply loved.

To my TEAM — you know who you are. You have walked with me through it all. You have supported me in caring for Billy. You have stood by me during my health challenges. You have called to check on me day and night. Some of you have even said you would ride six or seven hours just to help me recover if I needed you. That kind of loyalty and love does not go unnoticed. I love all of you more than words can say.

To the Freeman family — Andre, Kim, AJ, and Sydney — thank you for always making Raleigh feel like home. You are my hotel and motel whenever I am in town! You take care of your brother/Uncle Phil like no other. I love you all so much.

To my Celebration Church of Columbia family — you have been my spiritual foundation for over 18 years. The Men of Celebration often quote 1 Corinthians 16:13–14:

> "Be on your guard; stand firm in the faith; be courageous; be strong. Do everything in love."

Celebration Church, you have shown me nothing but love. For that, I am forever grateful.

And to Billy A. Lanier — Bro. You showed me tough love when I was at my lowest. Sometimes in my dreams, I revisit our conversations and the places we've been. As we tell this story, I acknowledge you today — not perfect all the time, but always rooted in love and respect for one another.

ABOUT THE AUTHOR

Raised in Clayton, North Carolina, in Johnston County, Phillip Mitchell was shaped by strong family roots and the values of small-town life that continue to guide him today. A devoted Christian, he strives to live with faith, integrity, and compassion in all that he does. His relationship with God is central to his life and influences the way he leads, serves, and supports those around him.

Phillip is a proud graduate of Saint Augustine's University, where he developed both his academic foundation and a lifelong commitment to leadership and service. He is also a dedicated member of Alpha Phi Alpha Fraternity, Inc., an organization that reflects his commitment to brotherhood, scholarship, and community impact.

Above all, Phillip is a devoted father of two, a role he considers his greatest blessing and responsibility. He is also a committed brother and loyal family member who believes that family is the foundation of strength. Known for his positive spirit and uplifting presence, Phillip approaches life with optimism and determination. A hardworking and loyal friend, he consistently shows up with purpose, encouragement, and a heart focused on making a meaningful difference.